Little People, **BIG DREAMS**

L. M. MONTGOMERY

Written by
Mª Isabel Sánchez Vegara

Illustrated by
Anuska Allepuz

Lincoln
Children's Books

Little Maud was born on Prince Edward Island, in Canada. When she was very small, her mother passed away. Her father left her in the care of her grandparents, and sailed off, faraway from the little island.

Maud felt out of place at her grandparents' house.
They were strict and grumpy and it was almost
impossible to get a smile out of them.

But Maud loved to walk around the island picking berries and naming everything she saw. For her, even apple trees had names like Little Syrup, Gavin or Spider.

At home, books became Maud's very best friends and she dreamt of becoming a writer one day. But her grandparents thought reading and writing was a waste of time, especially for a girl!

So, Maud started writing her own stories and poems in secret, smuggling candles into her room at night. She thought about the friends she'd found on her walks, and imagined new worlds for them.

When Maud was older, she became a teacher.
It was not her favourite job, but it gave her
time to write stories. And soon, one
was published in a magazine!

Maud was then offered the chance to work at a newspaper.
She was the only woman on the staff and wrote her
first article under the pen name: 'Cynthia'.
She loved every minute of her job!

But not even nine months had passed in her new post, when her grandfather passed away. Maud had to go back home to take care of her elderly grandmother.

But there was no way Maud would give up writing!
She accepted a job at the local post office, so she could
send her work to newspapers without anyone noticing.
Before long, thirty of her stories were in the papers.

One day, Maud found an old newspaper with an interesting story. It said: 'elderly couple apply to orphan asylum for a boy. By mistake, a girl is sent to them'. That night, she dreamt of this little girl…

... Who became the star of Maud's next story, *Anne of Green Gables*. Once it was published, everyone loved the little girl, with her freckles and thick red plaits.

Anne was imaginative, brave, and though she got into scrapes, she was always loved. Through Anne's adventures, Maud rewrote her own childhood as she'd have liked it to be.

And by telling Anne's story, Maud – the little girl who wasn't allowed to write – became the great author she always dreamt she could be.

L. M. MONTGOMERY

(Born 1874 • Died 1942)

c. 1883   c. 1888

Lucy Maud Montgomery was born in a small wooden house on
Prince Edward Island, in Canada. Although her name was Lucy,
she preferred to be called 'Maud – without the "e"'. When Maud
was one, her mother became ill and passed away. Her father
then moved west to the mainland, and sent Maud to live with her
grandparents, in the north of the island. Maud's childhood was
lonely, as her grandparents showed her little affection or attention.
So, she found solace through books, writing and her imagination.
When she was nine, she started writing poetry and journals. By the
time she was a teenager, she was already publishing short stories in
newspapers throughout North America. As an adult, Maud moved

c. 1902   1935

around, working as a teacher, and at a newspaper, but had to return
home to care for her grandmother. Then one day, she was inspired by
a newspaper story about a couple who adopted a child. They wanted
a boy but were sent a girl instead. Maud wrote a novel based on
this idea, calling it *Anne of Green Gables*. At first, it was rejected by
every publisher. So she kept it in a hat box and forgot about it. Then,
two years later, she tried again. The book found its home and was
published to great success: everyone fell in love with Anne. Maud had
created one of the most charming characters children's literature had
ever seen. Maud went on to write 14 novels, and became one of the
best-loved authors in Canada – and all over the world.

Want to find out more about **L. M. Montgomery?**
Have a read of these great books:

Anne of Green Gables by L. M. Montgomery
House of Dreams: The Life of L. M. Montgomery
by Liz Rosenberg and Julie Morstad

If you're in Canada, you could even visit the house where Maud was born, in
Clifton, on Prince Edward Island.

Brimming with creative inspiration, how-to projects, and useful
information to enrich your everyday life, Quarto Knows is a favourite
destination for those pursuing their interests and passions. Visit our
site and dig deeper with our books into your area of interest:
Quarto Creates, Quarto Cooks, Quarto Homes, Quarto Lives,
Quarto Drives, Quarto Explores, Quarto Gifts, or Quarto Kids.

Text © 2018 Mª Isabel Sánchez Vegara. Illustrations © 2018 Anuska Allepuz.

First Published in the UK in 2018 by Lincoln Children's Books, an imprint of The Quarto Group.
The Old Brewery, 6 Blundell Street, London N7 9BH, United Kingdom.
T (0)20 7700 6700 F (0)20 7700 8066 **www.QuartoKnows.com**
First Published in Spain in 2018 under the title Pequeña & Grande L. M. Montgomery
by Alba Editorial, s.l.u., Baixada de Sant Miquel, 1, 08002 Barcelona
www.albaeditorial.es

A catalogue record for this book is available from the British Library.
ISBN 978-1-78603-295-9

The illustrations were created with pencils, ink and engraving techniques (monotype and linocut).
Set in Futura BT.

Published by Rachel Williams • Designed by Karissa Santos
Edited by Katy Flint • Production by Jenny Cundill

Manufactured in Guangdong, China CC092018

9 7 5 3 1 2 4 6 8

Photographic acknowledgements (pages 28-29, from left to right) 1. L. M. Montgomery age 9 © L. M. Montgomery Collection, University of
Guelph 2. L. M. Montgomery age 14 © L. M. Montgomery Collection, University of Guelph 3. L. M. Montgomery frontispiece of diary, age 28 ©
L. M. Montgomery Collection, University of Guelph 4. L. M. Montgomery age 61, 1935 © L. M. Montgomery Collection, University of Guelph

Collect the *Little People*, **BIG DREAMS** series:

FRIDA KAHLO

ISBN: 978-1-84780-770-0

COCO CHANEL

ISBN: 978-1-84780-771-7

MAYA ANGELOU

ISBN: 978-1-84780-890-5

AMELIA EARHART

ISBN: 978-1-84780-885-1

AGATHA CHRISTIE

ISBN: 978-1-84780-959-9

MARIE CURIE

ISBN: 978-1-84780-961-2

ROSA PARKS

ISBN: 978-1-78603-017-7

AUDREY HEPBURN

ISBN: 978-1-78603-052-8

EMMELINE PANKHURST

ISBN: 978-1-78603-019-1

ELLA FITZGERALD

ISBN: 978-1-78603-086-3

ADA LOVELACE

ISBN: 978-1-84780-075-7

JANE AUSTEN

ISBN: 978-1-78603-119-8

GEORGIA O'KEEFFE

ISBN: 978-1-78603-121-1

HARRIET TUBMAN

ISBN: 978-1-78603-289-8

ANNE FRANK

ISBN: 978-1-78603-292-8

MOTHER TERESA

ISBN: 978-1-78603-290-4

JOSEPHINE BAKER

ISBN: 978-1-78603-291-1

L. M. MONTGOMERY

ISBN: 978-1-78603-295-9

JANE GOODALL

ISBN: 978-1-78603-294-2

SIMONE DE BEAUVOIR
ISBN: 978-1-78603-293-5

Now in board book format:

COCO CHANEL

ISBN: 978-1-78603-246-1

MAYA ANGELOU

ISBN: 978-1-78603-250-8

FRIDA KAHLO

ISBN: 978-1-78603-248-5

AMELIA EARHART

ISBN: 978-1-78603-251-5

MARIE CURIE

ISBN: 978-1-78603-254-6